CW01337017

THE 12th ROYAL LANCERS IN FRANCE

AUGUST 17th, 1914—NOVEMBER 11th, 1918

OFFICERS 12TH ROYAL LANCERS WHO SAILED FOR FRANCE, AUGUST, 1914.

Taken at Norwich.

Back Row.—Lieut. Spicer, Lieut. Wroughton (killed), Lieut. Eden (killed), Lieut. Brand, Lieut. Richardson, Lieut. Nicholas, Lieut. Leatham (killed), Lieut. Charrington, Capt. Bryant, Lieut. Moore, Lieut. Styles, Lieut. Leche, Lieut. Wernher, Lieut. Wyndham-Quin, and Lieut. Boden

Front Row.—Lieut. Brooke-Knop, Capt. Murray (killed), Major Macnaghten, Major Crawley (killed), Lieut.-Col. Wormald (killed), Major Bailey, Major Fane, and Capt. Micheli (killed).

THE 12TH ROYAL LANCERS IN FRANCE

AUGUST 17TH 1914—NOVEMBER 11TH 1918

by

MAJOR H. V. S. CHARRINGTON, M.C.

The Naval & Military Press Ltd

Reproduced by kind permission of the Central Library,
Royal Military Academy, Sandhurst

Published by
The Naval & Military Press Ltd
Unit 10, Ridgewood Industrial Park,
Uckfield, East Sussex,
TN22 5QE England
Tel: +44 (0) 1825 749494
Fax: +44 (0) 1825 765701
www.naval-military-press.com
www.military-genealogy.com
© The Naval & Military Press Ltd 2007

The Naval & Military Press ...

...offer specialist books for the serious student of conflict. The range of titles stocked covers the whole spectrum of military history with titles on uniforms, battles, official histories, specialist works containing Medal Rolls and Casualties Lists, and numismatic titles for medal collectors and researchers.

The innovative approach they have to military bookselling and their commitment to publishing have made them Britain's leading independent military bookseller.

In reprinting in facsimile from the original, any imperfections are inevitably reproduced and the quality may fall short of modern type and cartographic standards.

Printed and bound by CPI Antony Rowe, Eastbourne

TO THE UNDYING MEMORY

OF THE

OFFICERS, NON-COMMISSIONED OFFICERS AND MEN

OF THE

12TH ROYAL LANCERS

WHO GAVE THEIR LIVES FOR THEIR

COUNTRY THIS SMALL RECORD OF

THEIR ACHIEVEMENTS IS HUMBLY

DEDICATED.

FOREWORD

BY LT.-GEN. SIR PHILIP CHETWODE, BART., K.C.B., K.C.M.G., D.S.O.,

DEPUTY CHIEF OF THE IMPERIAL GENERAL STAFF.

May 2nd, 1921.

MY DEAR CHARRINGTON,

I am very glad you have written some small account of the doings of your distinguished regiment in the Great War. Such books are not only very much appreciated both by those who served and those who lost relatives in the war, but will also be of great use to future historians.

I have read it with great interest, and I have only two faults to find with it: one is that it is so short, and another that it is so modest.

No one knows better than I do how splendidly the regiment behaved whenever it was in action, and I feel that many of the battles and actions to which you refer in almost as brief terms as a war diary are deserving of more detailed treatment, just as those who fought in them are most assuredly deserving of all praise and honour for their conduct in them.

I have always thought, for instance, that the part played by the Cavalry in October and early November, 1914, has never been done full justice to, and most assuredly the 12th Lancers did their share, and more than their share, during that critical time.

I shall always be intensely proud of having had the regiment under my command for the first two years of the war in the 5th Cavalry Brigade and the 2nd Cavalry Division.

Yours sincerely,

(Signed) PHILIP W. CHETWODE.

THE 12th ROYAL LANCERS IN FRANCE

AUGUST 17th, 1914—NOVEMBER 11th, 1918

On the outbreak of war, August 4th, 1914, the Regiment, commanded by Lieut.-Colonel F. Wormald, was stationed at Norwich, with an outlying squadron ("C") at Weedon. Mobilization took place at Norwich, and on August 16th the Regiment entrained for Southampton, and landed at Havre on the following day with 25 officers, 523 other ranks, and 608 horses. Two days later it entrained for Hautmont, just outside Maubeuge, around which fortress the British Expeditionary Force was concentrating prior to moving forward into Belgium.

On the 21st the forward move began, and the Regiment moved for the first time as part of the 5th Cavalry Brigade, under the command of General Sir Philip Chetwode, Bart., the other regiments composing the Brigade being the 20th Hussars and the Royal Scots Greys; and these three regiments fought together as the 5th Cavalry Brigade throughout the war.

On August 22nd our leading patrols came into contact with the enemy in the vicinity of Binche, but although on the 23rd a patrol under 2nd-Lieut. Brand, in a midnight encounter with the Germans in the thick woods around Merbes-Ste.-Marie, lost one of their number—Cpl. London, who was the first 12th Lancer to be killed in the war—it was not till August 24th that the whole Regiment received their baptism of fire. On this day the task of the Brigade was to cover the right flank of the 1st Corps in their retirement from Mons, and the Regiment took up its position in front of the villages of Harveng and Novelles. They were heavily shelled throughout most of the day, but fought their way steadily back, losing one man killed and one officer and three men wounded, and with the remainder of the Brigade kept the Germans well back, so that the infantry they were covering were able to retire almost unmolested. Throughout the next six days the task of the Brigade was to cover the retirement of our infantry, and the Regiment was almost continually engaged in fighting rearguard actions, moving out at dawn through the infantry outposts, and not coming in behind them again till after dusk, which entailed long weary night marches through unknown country, often not reaching the allotted bivouacs till midnight, so that by the time horses had been watered and fed, a meal cooked and eaten, and rations drawn and issued for the next day, it was practically time to move off again. Luckily, the weather was fine and warm, and the country full of ripe oats and splendid fruit trees, so that, in spite of the very little rest they got, both men and horses kept surprisingly fit, though by the morning of the 28th, after six consecutive days of rearguard fighting, they were both somewhat exhausted. On the evening of the 25th a troop of "C" Squadron, under Lieut. R. S. T. Moore, was cut off and surrounded on the northern edge of the Foret de Mormal. Lieut. R. S. T. Moore and eleven men were taken prisoners, but not before the greater number of the troop were killed and Lieut. R. S. T. Moore and the remainder had all been wounded. On the afternoon of the 28th, while the Brigade was resting near the village of Moy on the Oise, a German Cavalry Brigade attempted to push through the outposts of the Royal Scots Greys, who were covering the

Brigade during its halt. The Brigade was quickly saddled up, and attacked at once, a very spirited action following, in which "C" Squadron of the Regiment made a most successful charge, killing seventy Germans outright with their lances, and taking several prisoners, while the fire from "A" and "B" Squadrons, who were covering their charge, dismounted, together with the action of the Royal Scots Greys and 20th Hussars and the good shooting of "J" Battery, inflicted such heavy casualties upon the enemy that this German Brigade was not fit to take the field again for a long time. Our total casualties were only one officer and four men killed, and Lieut.-Colonel F. Wormald and 5 men wounded. A full account of this action will be found in Appendix I at the end of the book. As a result of this engagement and of a fine stand made by the French on our right at Guise, the German pressure on our immediate front relaxed considerably, and the retirement was continued almost unmolested until the evening of September 5th, when the longed-for order to turn and attack the next day along the whole line was at last received. The Regiment moved out at dawn the following morning to the village of Pezarches, with orders to push patrols forward as far as Coulommiers if possible; but the German rearguard put up a very strong resistance, and, despite a heavy day's fighting, it was not till that evening that any real progress was made. Throughout the following day, when the Brigade captured Rebais, and for the ensuing week, the Germans were steadily pushed back to the Aisne, the Brigade being in action nearly every day, and the Regiment on September 10th playing a very prominent part in a most successful action fought around the villages of Chezy and Gandelu, in which a German convoy was surprised and over 300 prisoners taken, besides a large number of wagons full of stores, the Regiment's casualties being only five men killed and one officer and eight men wounded. On the following day the Regiment was visited by the Commander-in-Chief, General Sir John French, and warmly congratulated by him on its good work throughout the past three weeks. On September 12th the cavalry reached the Aisne, and on the 14th, after the infantry had forced a crossing, the Regiment was pushed across at Vailly, but was unable to debouch, and had a most unpleasant return passage across the two canal bridges; but, although these were continually swept by shell fire, casualties were surprisingly few.

That evening the Brigade was withdrawn and the Regiment billeted in the chateau and village of Couvrelles, where the battle, having now developed into trench warfare, it remained in reserve and enjoyed a welcome fortnight's rest.

The great northward move of the British forces was now to begin; in its original design it was an attempt to prolong the left of the French line about Arras and turn the German right, but it was soon to resolve itself, once Antwerp had fallen, into a desperate struggle to protect the Channel ports and maintain an unbroken line as far as the Belgian coast. The infantry divisions were withdrawn from the line and entrained as far as Hazebrouck and St. Omer, while the cavalry marched up. The Regiment left Couvrelles on September 30th, and commenced its march up to Flanders the following day. On October 10th the cavalry were in touch with German cavalry patrols just north of Aire. The 5th Cavalry Brigade, together with the 3rd and 4th Brigades, had now been formed into the 2nd Cavalry Division, and with the 1st Cavalry Division on their right the two divisions were now advancing in line. On October 12th the 2nd Cavalry Division occupied the Mont des Cats, the 3rd Cavalry Brigade driving a strong German cavalry force off this important position with great dash. During the next two days the Division drove the

German cavalry right back to the River Lys, occupying such important positions as the Mont Noir, Kemmel, and the Wytschaete—Messines ridge, without the possession of which it is very doubtful if our thin line could have held in the fierce fighting that was soon to follow.

Fighting in this enclosed country, with its high and wired hedges, its numerous by-roads and numberless farms and villages, was a very different and far more deadly affair than over the open rolling downlands we had fought over in August and September; but the skilful and bold way in which our patrols worked forward proved too much for the German cavalry and cyclists opposing us, and in the majority of cases they evacuated these important positions without a struggle. The Regiment itself occupied Mont Noir, Kemmel, and the Scherpenberg on the 14th, and that evening the division linked up with the 3rd Cavalry Division, who, with the 7th Infantry Division, had recently landed at Ostend, and from that moment the allied line, thin as it was, ran continuously to the Belgian coast. Throughout the next few days an attempt was made to force the passage of the Lys, and the Regiment was engaged continuously; but it was soon realized that it would be all we could do to hold the ground already gained, and trenches were hastily and improvisedly dug and horses sent back in rear. In these days the cavalry had no entrenching tools, and the bayonets which were issued about this time were the only implements the men had for the purpose, with the addition of the few odd tools they collected from any neighbouring farms. On October 22nd began those endless attacks on the British line which history was subsequently to know as the first Battle of Ypres, and the Regiment, together with every other unit of the British Expeditionary Force, played its part in that magnificent but desperate defence.

For more than three weeks, with no reserves of any sort, practically no artillery, and with units so reduced by casualties that almost every man was in the front line, the British Army withstood the furious attacks of not less than ten times their numbers. With a preponderance of artillery fire such as had then never been dreamed of, the Germans launched corps after corps of fresh and brave troops in a desperate attempt to break through to the coast, but they failed, though when the last attack was beaten off not one-third of the defenders remained unwounded.

For twelve of these days the Cavalry Corps, consisting of six weak cavalry brigades (the 3rd Cavalry Division was acting independently), assisted by an infantry brigade from the Indian Corps, held over seven miles of line ; and at 3 a.m. on the last of these days, November 1st, the 12th Lancers, exhausted and weakened as they were, counter-attacked, and, assisted by a squadron of the 20th Hussars and a battalion of the Lincolns, retook the greater part of the village of Wytschaete with the bayonet, inflicting very heavy casualties upon the enemy. In the words of the Commander-in-Chief himself, this moment was perhaps the most critical of the whole battle ; the French Corps who were coming to our assistance were still some distance off ; the right of the Cavalry Corps line had been driven off the greater part of the ridge, and had not the German advance been checked during those fateful hours, the French would have arrived too late. Kemmel Hill would have fallen, and the road to the coast would have been open to the Germans.

During these days the Regiment suffered heavily both in officers and men, but after being withdrawn for a few days on November 3rd it was soon in the line again, and with the remainder of the Cavalry Corps spent the rest of the month in support of the French troops who had now taken over

ZILLEBEKE WOODS, FEBRUARY, 1915.

Capt. Osborne, 20th Hussars. Lt. Osmonde-Williams, Royal Scots Greys. Lt.-Col. Wormald. Brig.-Gen. Sir P. Chetwode, Comdg. 5th Cav. Bde. Major Truman. Capt. Charrington.

our line. Either hurrying to support some threatened position of the front, or occupying a sector of the front line to relieve some of the tired troops there, both men and horses got little rest, and the bitter wet and cold of a Flemish winter having now set in, it was a welcome day when the German attacks, now having completely ceased, the Cavalry Corps was withdrawn, and the Regiment went into billets around Steenwerck at the beginning of December.

The Brigade remained in the Steenwerck area till the beginning of January, 1915, when a welcome move was made to the neighbourhood of Fauquembergues, the Regiment being allotted the villages of Wandonne and Audinchthun. Only four farms had been allotted to the whole Regiment while it remained around Steenwerck, so that all the horses were in the open, and the men terribly overcrowded ; but in the new area plenty of buildings were available, and both men and horses were much better off. It was not, however, to be for long, as early in February the Brigade moved to the Merville area, the Regiment occupying billets around Caudescure, and being destined to occupy the very same billets on several more occasions during the following two years. Training in the use of bombs and trench mortars, both of a somewhat crude pattern, was now commenced, and on February 13th, leaving the horses in billets, with one man to look after four, the Regiment went up to Ypres in motor buses, the Cavalry Corps having taken over a sector of the line in the Zillebeke Woods, so as to give some of the tired infantry battalions an opportunity for rest. The Regiment had a fairly quiet time during its seven days' tour in the front line, as, owing to the opposing trenches being in thick pine-woods and very close together, neither side could shell the opposing front-line trenches without great risk to their own men. There was a good deal of sniping, however, in which the Regiment more than held its own, but nevertheless had a good many casualties ; and the men also suffered a good deal from the wet, most of the trenches being waterlogged.

The enemy blew a mine under a portion of trench just on the Regiment's left, held by the 16th Lancers, and besides the casualties resulting from the explosion, this Regiment suffered very heavy casualties in an unsuccessful counter-attack to regain the mine crater which the Germans had immediately occupied. When in reserve the Regiment was billeted in the town of Ypres itself, which at that time was very little shelled, and as a number of good houses still remained undamaged all ranks were very comfortable there.

The Regiment returned to billets at the end of February, and after returning to the Fauquembergues area for four days, moved back again to Caudescure on March 9th.

The following day the Brigade moved up to Estaires, ready to follow up the infantry and push through to the Aubers ridge if the attack on Neuve Chapelle succeeded.

An order was received to push through on the evening of the 12th, but it was soon realized that mounted troops could not possibly get forward, as the German resistance was by no means broken, so the order was quickly cancelled and the following morning the Brigade was withdrawn, the Regiment returned to Caudescure, where it remained until April 23rd. On this day the Brigade was hurried up to Vlamertinghe in support of our hard-pressed troops in the Ypres salient. This was now in great danger of capture, as the French line on the north of the salient had completely given way as a result of a fierce German attack on the morning of the 21st preceded by clouds of poison gas. This was the first appearance of this terrible method of offence, and against troops unfurnished with anti-gas appliances of any description its effect was annihilating.

"B" SQUADRON FRONT LINE, ZILLEBEKE WOODS, FEBRUARY, 1915.

Leaving the horses at Vlamertinghe, the Brigade moved up dismounted to occupy a reserve line running just east of the town, the portion of it allotted to the Brigade running from the village of Potije to the Halte on the Menin road. The march up, skirting the southern outskirts of the town and moving up the railway cutting on the Ypres—Roulers railway, was an uncomfortable one, as the town and railway cutting were being heavily shelled; but by moving in small parties at wide intervals the line was eventually reached and occupied without much loss. Once there, a busy week was spent deepening and improving the line, and although the Germans shelled the town continuously with guns of all calibres and the ration limbers had an adventurous journey through it every night, the trenches themselves were very little shelled, and there were very few casualties.

On May 3rd the Brigade returned to the horses at Vlamertinghe and moved back to the Merville area, with the intention of co-operating if the attacks by the 1st Army were successful. At 2 a.m. on May 14th, however, the situation in the Ypres salient again being critical, horses were left in billets, and the Brigade hurried up in motor buses to Vlamertinghe. The same evening it marched up through Ypres and took over a portion of the front line about Verlorenhoek from the 3rd Cavalry Division, who had suffered terribly severe casualties there on the two preceding days. The Brigade held this sector for a week, during which time the Germans made no further serious attack, but the Regiment suffered a good many casualties from shelling and sniping, amongst others Major (now Lieut.-Colonel) C. Fane, D.S.O., being severely wounded.

On May 21st the Brigade was withdrawn to Vlamertinghe, but moved up again on the evening of the 24th, and occupied the ramparts of the eastern edge of Ypres, where it remained in reserve for another ten days. The machine-gun sections of the three regiments were sent up to reinforce the 3rd Cavalry Brigade, who were having a very rough time just south of Hooge, and on May 28th the Regimental machine guns played a prominent part in repulsing a German attack on Hooge village, inflicting heavy losses on the attackers. On May 30th the machine guns were withdrawn and the Brigade returned to its horses, and on June 1st the Regiment left Caudescure for a new billeting area on the edge of the forest of Clairmarais, remaining there till the beginning of August. During this time strong parties were sent up to dig and prepare defensive works around La Clytte. In July General Sir Philip Chetwode, Bart., was promoted to the command of the 2nd Cavalry Division, and Lieut.-Colonel F. Wormald given command of the 5th Cavalry Brigade, Major Macnaughten succeeding him in command of the Regiment. At the beginning of August the Regiment moved to new billets around Racquinghem. Early in September the working parties were withdrawn, and after a fortnight's mounted training the Division moved on September 21st, to co-operate with the 1st Army if their attack on the German line around Loos afforded an opportunity.

The Regiment billeted at Estree-Blanche, Hestrus, and Cauchy-La-Tour on its march there, remaining at this last-named small mining village throughout the battle, in which, although Loos and a large portion of the German front-line system was captured, no opportunity for its employment occurred. On September 29th, all hopes of using cavalry having vanished, the Brigade was withdrawn, and the Regiment went into its billets in Fontaine-les-Hermans. During the first week in October a dismounted party was sent up from the Division to clear up the battlefield, and while in command of this party Brigadier-General F. Wormald was unfortunately killed by a shell, his body being brought back and buried at Nedonchelle.

At the end of October the Cavalry Corps was sent into winter quarters, the Regiment being allotted the villages of Campagne-les-Boulonnais and Happe, and remaining there till the beginning of 1916. During this time it furnished digging parties for work on a reserve line around Le Nieppe, and wood-cutting parties to work in the forests near Lumbres. So great had been the casualties among infantry officers in the recent fighting, that the cavalry were now asked for volunteers to replace them. A very large number of officers and N.C.Os. offered themselves, but only a very limited number could be spared. Major C. Truman was given command of the 1/6th Black Watch, and eight N.C.Os. from the Regiment were given commissions in various infantry battalions.

At different periods later on various N.C.Os. from the Regiment were given commissions, and almost without exception proved themselves the most valuable and gallant officers, perhaps the most noteworthy among many fine performances being that of Sgt. Smeltzer, who within two years of first receiving his commission was not only commanding his battalion, but had also gained the D.S.O. and bar and the M.C., besides other honours. The Cavalry Corps were also given a regular dismounted organization for trench warfare, each Cavalry Brigade providing a dismounted battalion and each regiment finding a dismounted company, battalion headquarters being furnished by the regiments in turn. This was a great improvement on the old system, in which far too great a proportion of officers and senior N.C.Os. had always gone into the trenches compared to the proportion of these ranks in an infantry battalion in the line.

On January 2nd, 1916, the Cavalry Corps having again taken over a sector of the line from the 1st Army, the dismounted company from the Regiment, consisting of 15 officers and 372 other ranks, was sent up to the neighbourhood of Vermelles, remaining there for nearly six weeks, during part of which time the Regiment also furnished battalion headquarters. Although the sector was a so-called quiet one, and no active operations on a large scale were carried out by either side, there was a great deal of mining and counter-mining on both sides, which meant hard fighting for the possession of the mine craters and constant sniping and bombing attacks, so that, although there were not many casualties, it was an anxious and hard-working time for all ranks.

On the dismounted company returning to the horses, training at once began in the use of Hotchkiss guns. One of these excellent weapons was now given to each troop, and was to prove itself an invaluable addition to its fire power throughout the remainder of the war. Machine-gun detachments were now taken away from regiments, and machine-gun squadrons formed in each brigade, Captain D. C. H. Richardson being given command of the 5th Cavalry Brigade Squadron.

The Regiment remained at Campagne-les-Boulonnais till the beginning of April, when a move was made to Bonningues, where the Brigade did a fortnight's mounted training over a large area of ground in the vicinity which had been rented for this purpose. It then returned to Campagne-les-Boulonnais for another fortnight, and moved again early in May to the pleasant villages of Tournehem, Zouafques, and Nordausques, all situated on the edge of the training area.

The remainder of the month was spent in carrying out Divisional, Brigade, and Regimental schemes over the ground, in all of which the main idea was to practise mounted operations such as cavalry would be called upon to carry out once the enemy's trench system had been broken through.

This last possibility being always known to any cavalryman as a "Gap."

At the beginning of June the dismounted company was sent up to the Ypres sector, where, the situation again being doubtful, the whole of the 2nd Cavalry Division dismounted battalions were placed under the orders of the Second Army. They were, however, only required to dig and improve reserve lines, and returned after a fortnight. A few days later the 2nd Cavalry Division moved to the Merville area, the Regiment returning to its old billets around Caudescure. It remained there till the beginning of September, strong digging parties being found all the time for work near Locre and Neuve Eglise. They did a lot of good work, making railways, burying cables, and digging gun emplacements in preparation for the Second Army's projected attack on the Messines Ridge, which was, however, not destined to take place till nearly a year later. The digging parties were withdrawn at the beginning of September, and on the 6th inst. the Division commenced its march down to the Somme, where a big offensive by the British and French had been in progress since the beginning of July.

The Regiment billeted at Lozinghem, Pierremont, Le Ponchel, Occoches, Naours, and Bonnay on its march down, reaching its bivouacs near the village of Bray-sur-Somme on September 14th. The following morning the Division stood to in readiness to co-operate if a big infantry attack, which began at dawn, made sufficient progress. In this attack, in which tanks were most successfully used, this being their first appearance on any battlefield, much ground was gained, but the German resistance was by no means broken, and the whole battlefield was so ploughed up by shell-fire, and in such a water-logged state, that any idea of employing cavalry had to be abandoned.

The Division remained in bivouacs around Bray till the beginning of October, finding large digging parties to work on roads and trenches in the forward area, and saddling up and standing to during all the numerous infantry attacks. The weeks of wet weather and the continuous heavy shelling had now made the battlefield an almost impassable sea of mud, so that even had the German line given way, which on several occasions it seemed on the point of doing, it would have been an immense task to get even the smallest body of horsemen forward. On October 2nd the whole Division was withdrawn to the neighbourhood of Morlancourt, one squadron only being sent forward to support each fresh infantry attack, but despite almost superhuman efforts by the infantry, each attack only gained a few hundred yards, and after the most bitter fighting no opportunity even for the employment of one squadron ever offered itself.

At Morlancourt the Regiment had its lines on the slopes of the hill just north-east of the village. The camp was terribly exposed, and it rained ceaselessly throughout the whole month it remained there, so that the lines soon became a muddy swamp. A few tents were available, and enough rough shelter was made out of any material that could be found to provide cover for all the men, but the horses were in the open all the time and suffered terribly. Digging parties were found throughout the month for work on the forward area, but though they had a rough time, and suffered a certain number of casualties, all ranks could only feel ashamed at the very small part they could play in this great battle, in which the infantry, besides fighting almost without a break, were undergoing untold hardships and discomfort in the oceans of mud which the ever-changing front line had developed into.

On November 7th the Division was withdrawn, and it

was a very sorry-looking lot of horses and a very dirty collection of men that represented the 12th Lancers as they gladly filed out of "Mud-camp" that morning. The Division now went into winter quarters, the Regiment marching via Bussy-les-Daours, Yzeux, and Drucat to Auchy-les-Hesdin, where both men and horses were well housed, and the inhabitants most friendly. Just before leaving the Somme General Greenly, an old 12th Lancer, had succeeded Major-General Sir Philip Chetwode, Bart., in command of the 2nd Cavalry Division, and Lieut.-Colonel C. Fane, D.S.O., having returned, assumed command of the Regiment. The Regiment remained at Auchy-les-Hesdin throughout the winter of 1916-1917, finding working parties to help in the construction of a new railway-line to Arras, and carrying out a lot of training in dispatch riding, patrolling, and the employment of Hotchkiss guns. The winter was an exceptionally severe one, the coldest experienced during the campaign, and though officers and men were very comfortable indeed in Auchy and the outlying villages, the horses, whose ration had now been reduced to only 7 lbs. of oats, began to lose condition with alarming rapidity. This reduction was unavoidable owing to the serious deficiency in ships caused by the heavy losses from the campaign of unrestricted submarine warfare which the Germans had just initiated, and against which for the first few months we had practically no counter-measures. But its result was that the horses, whose ration was now barely enough to keep them alive and not nearly enough to enable them to stand long exercise or the rigours of a hard winter, were totally unfitted for the long marches and exposure they were called upon to face in April. At the beginning of this month the working parties were withdrawn, and a strong dismounted party sent up to Arras to prepare a track along which cavalry could move forward as the attack progressed.

Our offensive in this sector had been in preparation throughout the winter, and the most minute and careful arrangements had been made to ensure its success. The 5th Cavalry Brigade concentrated on April 5th, the Regiment marching to Remaisnil, whence on Easter Sunday, April 8th, it moved to some huts between Grincourt and Pas. The day was a bright and warm one, but the following morning, on which our offensive began at dawn, was bitterly cold, wet and windy, and snow fell heavily in the afternoon. The attack was most successful, our troops in front of Arras completely overrunning the first two German lines, and taking numbers of prisoners, our casualties being surprisingly few; at the same time the Canadian Corps on the left captured the Vimy Ridge, which for over two years had defied every attack.

The 5th Cavalry Brigade moved up during the afternoon through the outskirts of Arras along the cavalry track to Telegraph Hill. The cavalry dismounted party who had gone up to prepare the track had gone forward with the leading waves of the infantry, and, despite severe shelling from which they suffered many casualties, had prepared an excellent track in a few hours.

The infantry attack was unfortunately checked about Feuchy Chapel, and after remaining on Telegraph Hill till nightfall, the Brigade was ordered to withdraw to Wailly. It was pitch-dark, a blinding snowstorm had set in, and the track by that time had become a quagmire, so that it took the Regiment over seven hours to cover the four miles back to Wailly, and by the time they had reached there men and horses were very exhausted. Horses were pegged down in an open field, and officers and men laid down close beside them, getting what shelter they could from their saddles; but the snowstorm was so severe that several horses died of

TELEGRAPH HILL, APRIL 9TH, 1917—OFFICERS 12TH ROYAL LANCERS.

Lt. Davidge. Lt. McCreery. Lt. Ogilvy. Lt. Ford. Lt. Rawnsley. Lt. Freer. Lt. Straker. Lt. Vass. Capt. Davidson.
Lt. MacBean. Capt. Wyndham-Quin. Lt. Spicer. Lt. Hammond.

exposure during the night and a few men were badly frost-bitten. The next day, as the infantry attack was reported to be making good progress, the Brigade was again ordered forward, and, moving off about midday, advanced along the track over Telegraph Hill through Tilloy to just west of the village of Wancourt, where our leading infantry battalions had just captured the old German third line, but were unable to progress beyond it.

The 3rd and 5th Cavalry Brigades remained in this exposed position till the following morning, it being first hoped that there would be an opportunity for a mounted advance at dawn, and later, when it was realized that a strong German counter-attack was developing, it being considered that the withdrawal of the cavalry would dishearten the infantry, who were being very hard pressed. The 5th Cavalry Brigade, which was under direct observation from the Germans, suffered terribly severe casualties, being shelled continuously throughout the night, and when daylight broke leaving it in close formation in full view of the Germans, guns of all calibres, as well as machine-gun and rifle fire, were directed upon it until withdrawn about 8 a.m. The 12th Lancers, being rear regiment of the Brigade, and unfortunately the most exposed, suffered the heaviest casualties in the Division, 6 officers and 50 other ranks being killed and wounded, and over 100 horses killed, besides many more wounded. On the order being given to withdraw, the Regiment, despite its terrible hammering and getting the head of the column blown away just as it moved off, retired slowly to Tilloy without a trace of unsteadiness, and on arrival there immediately proceeded to reorganize its remnants with a view to further operations if required. The German counter-attack was, however, beaten off by the infantry, and about 4 p.m. the Brigade was withdrawn to Wailly, where the exhausted horses at last got water after being without it for nearly thirty-three hours. The following morning the Brigade marched back to the huts near Pas, remaining there for a week, during which time it rained ceaselessly, and the half-starved horses, many of which had already died from exposure, grew steadily thinner. A move was at last made back to better billets, and on April 20th the Regiment moved to an area just east of Auxi-le-Chateau, billeting in the villages of Beauvoir, Nœux, and Bealcourt. Fine weather now set in, and with men and horses well housed, and reinforcements of both coming up from the base, in a very few days the Regiment became an efficient fighting unit again.

The 2nd Cavalry Division remained in this area till the middle of May, when the Cavalry Corps again took over a sector of the line in the neighbourhood of Hargicourt. The Regiment marched via Bertaucourt, Querrieu, and Vaux, and thence across the Somme battlefield through Peronne to Tincourt, where horse lines were put down and dismounted company sent up to the trenches. The sector was a very quiet one, and during the two months the Brigade was in the line there were very few casualties except amongst the Royal Scots Greys, who were holding Guillemont Farm on our left, the possession of which important position was always in dispute. The Division was relieved on July 12th and sent up to the First Army area, the Regiment marching via Suzanne, Morlancourt, and Sarton to an area around Frevent. It was first billeted at Rebreuviette, but the billets there being very dirty and crowded, they moved a few days later to Mezerolles, with outlying squadrons at Le Meillard and Remaisnil. The Brigade remained in this area till the beginning of October, when it was moved to an area near St. Pol, with a view of co-operating in an offensive the First Army was carrying out. The Regiment billeted in the villages of

Hernicourt, Pierremont, and Wavrans. The wet weather which had now set in made any hope of employing cavalry in this low-lying country quite impossible, and after ten days in these billets the Brigade was moved southwards again, the Regiment marching via Vacquerie-les-Boucq and Bethencourt to the villages of Naumps-au-Mont, Taisnil, and Rumaisnil, about ten miles south of Amiens.

It remained there till the middle of November, when the Cavalry Corps was moved up by night marches to a concentration area east of Peronne about Montescourt to take part in the surprise attack on the German positions in front of Cambrai. The attack was delivered at dawn on November 20th, when, without any preliminary bombardment, but covered only by a creeping barrage, large numbers of our heavy tanks, accompanied by infantry, were launched against the German defences. The attack was a complete surprise, and this, the first employment of tanks on a large scale, most successful, a large portion of the famous Hindenburg Line being captured, the German positions penetrated very deeply, and large numbers of prisoners taken with very small losses on our side. Unfortunately, however, the full fruits of the initial victory were not reaped by the cavalry, the 1st Cavalry Division getting hung up the same afternoon south-east and east of Bourlon Wood, and owing to a tank going through the bridge over the canal at Masnieres, and no other means of crossing being discovered, the 3rd and 2nd Cavalry Divisions were unable to get forward and work round Cambrai from the south and east as had been originally intended.

The following day the Germans had railed up reinforcements, and all hopes of a break through vanished. We still, however, continued attacking, and on the 26th the Guards Division captured Bourlon Wood. The Germans at once counter-attacked, and so heavily did the various

Infantry Divisions defending the wood suffer, that the 2nd Cavalry Division were called upon to send up its dismounted battalions to assist in the defence. The dismounted company from the Regiment was entrusted with the defence of the north-east corner of the wood, and throughout the 28th and 29th November resisted every attack made upon them, and when withdrawn on the 29th, of the 5 officers and 164 men who went up, not a single officer and only 100 men returned to the horses, the remainder having all been killed or wounded. While they had been in Bourlon Wood, the remainder of the Regiment with the led horses had been concentrated on the edge of the Bois Dessarts, just north-east of Fins, and what was left of the dismounted company rejoined it there on the morning of the 30th. The following morning a surprise German attack enabled them to break through our front line on a fairly wide front, and penetrate as far as Gouzeaucourt, which was barely two miles from our bivouac. The Brigade was at once turned out, and working forward with the Guards Division on the left and the 4th Cavalry Division on the right, Gouzeaucourt was recaptured and the Germans pushed back beyond Gauche Wood.

The Regiment remained in mounted reserve throughout the day in the neighbourhood of Revelon Farm, the Royal Scots Greys and 20th Hussars being sent forward dismounted. About 4 p.m. " A " Squadron were ordered to try and work round Gouzeaucourt mounted, but they were soon stopped by wire and hostile fire, and had to return with a certain number of casualties.

Throughout the next four days the Brigade remained in this sector, horses being sent back to Dessarts Wood, and every available man sent either into support trenches around Revelon Farm or in working parties on the front line about Gauche Wood.

On December 5th, infantry reinforcements having arrived and the position being at last stabilized, the cavalry were withdrawn, and the Regiment, marching via Cartigny and Aubigny, moved to an area south-west of Amiens, where it billeted in the villages of Fricamps and Thieulloy l'Abbaye.

The Cavalry Corps were now placed under the orders of the Fifth Army, which had just taken over a large extent of front line from the French, and consequently held a very large extent of front very thinly and with practically no reserves. The dismounted battalions were therefore again sent up to the trenches, the 2nd Cavalry Division taking over a sector east and south-east of Hargicourt. The dismounted company from the Regiment left their horses at Fricamps on December 17th, and remained in the line till the end of January. Their portion of the line was known as Railway Trench, and ran just along the crest of Cologne Ridge.

The weather was bitterly cold and the ground covered with snow most of the time, so that beyond the usual shelling and sniping and an occasional raid in search of prisoners, no operations on a big scale were undertaken by either side, and there were very few casualties.

After returning to the horses, a few days were spent at Fricamps cleaning up, and on February 14th, 1918, the Regiment marched via Vers and Proyart, across the Somme at Brie, to Ennemain. The whole of the Cavalry Corps were now concentrated east of the Somme ready to support the Fifth Army if the expected German offensive was to fall upon any portion of the front it was holding.

At the beginning of March the 2nd Cavalry Division took over a portion of the front line east of Vermand, the dismounted company from the Regiment being in support in Vermand itself.

The Division was withdrawn after a week and moved

southwards to Quesmy, where it came under the orders of the 3rd Corps. On March 21st the long-expected German offensive began, the main weight of it falling upon our Fifth Army, who with only fourteen weak Divisions, extended over a front of some 42 miles, were now called upon to withstand the onslaught of 40 strong German Divisions, whose troops had been specially training throughout the winter for this offensive and were backed by an overwhelming preponderance of Artillery.

Despite a most determined resistance in most parts of the line, our battle positions were quickly penetrated, and the cavalry dismounted battalions were hurried up immediately to try and restore the situation. The battalion from the 5th Cavalry Brigade, containing the Regiment's dismounted company, was sent off about mid-day on the 21st to the support of the 14th Infantry Division about Jussy. They fought most gallantly, and on the 23rd did specially good work in covering the retirement of the 43rd Infantry Brigade near Faillouel. On the 24th the remnants of the battalion were mounted on horses, and, together with a collection of men from almost every cavalry regiment, were made into a composite force under General Harman, and did excellent work throughout the next two days in assisting the French troops west of Noyon to stop the German attempt to push southwards towards Compiègne. On March 23rd a troop was formed from the led-horse party of each regiment, and sent forward, joining General Harman's force on the 25th. The remainder of the led-horse party of the Brigade, with the assistance of some men from the Labour Corps, were got back through Noyon to Pontoise on the 23rd, and moved again on the 24th to Bailly, whence on the following morning a composite regiment was formed out of them, each regiment furnishing a squadron, which consisted mostly of N.C.Os.

and staff men. This composite regiment moved up to Pontoise, where a few remaining men from the original dismounted companies were collected and placed on horses, and such Hotchkiss and machine guns as they had been able to bring away with them were collected as well. It then moved up to Mont Renaud, south of Noyon, and the following day played a most effective part in assisting the French Divisions which had been hurried up to this sector to arrest the German advance about Dive-le-Franc and Suzoy, the force under General Harman being hotly engaged in the wooded country just west of these villages at the same time. Although the Germans were still sweeping westwards towards Montdidier and Amiens, their attempt to turn southwards on Compiègne was thus frustrated by the gallant sacrifices of the British Cavalry and the French Infantry Divisions in this sector, though their casualties had been terribly severe in so doing. On the 27th, the position in this sector being more or less secured, the cavalry were withdrawn, and the various detachments collected and sorted into regiments again, south of Compiègne. The following morning they were off again to Amiens, the fall of which seemed now almost certain. Despite the exhausted condition of men and horses, who had been continously fighting for nearly a week, the 2nd Cavalry Division arrived at Cagny, on the outskirts of Amiens, on the evening of March 29th, after two long and very trying marches, the total distance covered being over 50 miles. It was now immediately sent forward to the support of the few shattered infantry detachments that were attempting to cover the town, the 5th Cavalry Brigade being sent up to the Bois de L'Abbe.

On the afternoon of the 30th the Regiment was ordered to co-operate with the 9th Australian Infantry Brigade, who had just arrived from the First Army, in a counter-attack on the enemy north of Hangard Wood. The counter-attack was most successful, the line being completely restored, and the Germans pushed back several hundred yards. The reports on this action by the G.O.C. 9th Australian Infantry Brigade and G.O.C. 5th Cavalry Brigade will be found in Appendix II.

On the morning of April 1st the dismounted battalion from the Brigade took part in a counter-attack made by the 2nd Cavalry Division on Moreuil Wood, and the high ground to the north of it. The attack was most successful, this important ground being captured and held against the subsequent counter-attack, but the Division suffered very heavily. The following day, fresh infantry reinforcements having arrived, it was withdrawn to Camon on the outskirts of Amiens, and on April 6th, the safety of the town being now assured, was sent back to the neighbourhood of Abbeville to refit.

The Regiment marched to Yarcourt-Bussus, where a welcome reinforcement of 110 men, including 50 men from various Yeomanry Regiments, arrived to refill its depleted ranks. Its rest there was to be a very short one, as on April 9th the Germans commenced another big offensive on the First Army, their attack falling mainly upon the Portuguese troops, who were holding the line in front of Estaires.

Their line was quickly broken, and, the Germans following up their initial success with their usual skill, our Divisions on either flank were forced to withdraw, and the position again soon became critical. The cavalry were again hurried northwards, the Regiment marching via Guenne-Ivergny, Matringhem, and Blaringhem to the Forêt de Nieppe, where it remained in support for some days. Being not required, owing to the magnificent fighting of our infantry in this sector, particularly that of the 34th (Guards) Brigade, it was withdrawn to billets around Blaringhem. At the end of the month the Brigade moved to an area near Fauquembergues, the Regiment billeting in Radinghem. A week later the Brigade moved to an area between Hesdin and Montreuil, the Regiment being allotted the villages of Offin and Hesmond.

The Brigade remained in this area till the middle of July, a lot of mounted training and musketry being carried out; it was then sent up to Izel-les-Hameau, west of Arras, for a week, as a fresh German offensive was expected in this sector. The offensive did not develop, and the Regiment returned to Offin, where it remained till the beginning of August, when the whole of the Cavalry Corps was moved by night marches to the outskirts of Amiens, the Regiment marching via Le Boisée and Coulonvillers to Ailly-sur-Somme.

An attack on the German positions east of Amiens, in conjunction with a French offensive on our left, began at dawn on August 8th, and was an overwhelming success. Our concentration had been completely concealed from the enemy, and the heavy tanks and leading infantry divisions overran the German front-line defences before they could offer anything but the feeblest resistance.

The 1st and 3rd Cavalry Divisions with two battalions of whippet tanks were then pushed through, and penetrated to a depth of eight miles, only being stopped when they reached the old Somme battlefield, where the ground was almost impossible for cavalry or tanks to operate. Some 14,000 prisoners were taken and several hundred guns, and the moral of the whole German Army so shattered that this day's work proved to be the beginning of the end. The German soldier, who up till this had proved himself a most gallant and skilful enemy, never afterwards showed the same fighting qualities, and within less than three months the once great German Empire was compelled to sue for and accept an armistice, the conditions of which amounted to very little short of complete surrender. The 2nd Cavalry Division remained in reserve throughout this battle, an attempt to employ them on August 10th about Vrely not being successful. It was withdrawn on August 15th, and marched via St. Sauveur and Montrelet to the neighbourhood of Auxi-le-Chateau, the Regiment being billeted in Guenne-Ivergny. A few days later the 5th Cavalry Brigade was sent up to the Arras sector, where on the 23rd and 24th it was in support of the Third Army, who were now continuing the series of attacks on the German line, which Marshal Foch now in supreme command of the Allied Forces on the Western Front, had begun a few weeks previously. This attack made excellent progress, but the ground, which consisted mainly of old trenches, wire entanglements, and shell-holes, was most unfavourable for mounted action, and it was only possible to push forward small patrols. The Regiment furnished several of these, and in nearly every instance they did excellent work. Boldly and skilfully handled, they pushed well forward, obtaining much valuable information and sending in very good reports, which proved to be of the greatest assistance to the infantry. On August 26th the Regiment was placed under the orders of the 17th Corps, and for the following week was employed as Corps Cavalry during its successful attacks east of Arras, which culminated in the capture of the Drocourt-Queant switch, the last prepared German line of resistance in this sector. Owing to the nature of the ground over which the Corps was operating, there was no possibility of the Regiment being employed as a whole for mounted operations, and it therefore furnished troops to each of the infantry divisions, to act as dispatch riders, orderlies, etc., and other troops for police duties, or to escort prisoners, whilst the remainder of the Regiment was sent back to billets in Warluzel.

On September 1st the Regiment concentrated near Martin-sur-Cojeul, but as no opportunity for its employment occurred, it was withdrawn to Grincourt the following evening, where the 5th Cavalry Brigade was now concentrating again. A few days later the Brigade was placed under orders of the Fourth Army and moved southwards to an area around Querrieu, the Regiment billeting first in Frenchencourt and moving later to Molliens-au-Bois. The Brigade was then moved up to take part in the attack on the Hindenburg Line, and marching by night, via Morcourt and Le Mesnil Bruntel, concentrated on the morning of September 29th in the valley between Templeux-le-Guerard and Hargicourt—ground which had been so familiar to all ranks during their spells in the trenches in the summer of 1917, and again at Christmas of the same year. The attack, which was begun at dawn, met with splendid success on the right, where, despite the very thick fog, the 46th Division stormed the canal at Bellenglise and captured over 4,000 prisoners with less than a quarter of that number casualties. The two Australian Divisions, however, behind whom the Brigade was concentrated, were unable to pass through the two American Divisions in front of them as the American troops lost direction in the mist and never properly mopped up their first objectives, while more American Divisions on their left were bloodily repulsed in their attacks on Bony. The Australian Divisions, therefore, instead of pushing through the Americans and occupying the Masnieres-Beaurevoir line, as had been originally intended, had to be sent into the battle much earlier to clear up the somewhat ambiguous situation left by the Americans. They did this most gallantly and successfully, but by the time they had completed the task it was nearly nightfall and any hope of employing cavalry had vanished. Of the liaison party sent forward by the Brigade to keep it informed of the infantry situation, and which consisted of 2 officers and 5 men from the Regiment, only one officer returned unwounded from the whole party.

The Brigade was withdrawn to Roisel after dark, and the following day was placed under the orders of the 9th Corps, with which it co-operated for the next fortnight during its successful advance against the Fonsomme line and on to Bohain. The German resistance was still strong, and no opportunity for mounted action occurred, but the Regiment furnished mounted patrols throughout the fighting which did excellent work. The Brigade was left up in close support every day, ready to seize any opportunity which might occur, and as a result in front of Magny-la-Fosse, and later around Jonnecourt Farm and Mericourt, suffered a good many casualties from shell-fire, a hostile barrage which fell in the middle of the Regiment on October 2nd in the valley north-east of Magny-la-Fosse killing 1 officer and 1 man and wounding 5 officers and 14 men, and an attempt to get a Squadron forward mounted on October 8th in the operations around Mericourt resulting in 2 officers being severely wounded. On October 12th the Brigade was split up and the Regiment transferred to the 13th Corps, where it remained until the cessation of hostilities a month later.

It was first sent to Mont St. Martin, and after a few days moved to Maretz, whence on October 19th it was sent forward in support of an infantry attack on Pommerfuil and Casuel, south-east of Le Cateau. A few casualties were sustained amongst the advanced patrols, but there was no opportunity for a mounted advance and the Regiment was withdrawn to Maretz. On the 23rd it was again sent forward to White Springs, just north-east of Le Cateau, but the enclosed country on the edges of the Forêt de Mormal made a mounted advance impossible, and the Regiment was again withdrawn to Maretz.

On the evening of the 5th November the Regiment moved up again to a position of readiness east of Le Cateau. A strong attack by the British Third and Fourth Armies in connection with the French on our right commenced the following morning, and met with great success. In a very few hours Landrecies and the greater part of the Forêt de Mormal had been captured, and before nightfall the Regiment had moved forward through Landrecies and its leading patrols were engaged with the enemy well east and north-east of it. From now onwards, although their resistance, particularly that of their machine gunners, was still strong, the enemy were continually on the run, though their retirements were still well ordered. The Regiment furnished troops to each of the advanced brigades of the Corps, and the infantry, who were gaining ground daily, though not without hard fighting, found these troops invaluable for scouting and dispatch riding. The remainder of the Regiment followed close up, moving through Maroilles and Taisnieres (which latter village it had been the last to pass through on August 26th, 1914, on the retreat from Mons, and which, strangely enough, it was now to be the first British Regiment to enter on the morning of November 7th, 1918). From Taisnieres the Regiment moved to Dompierre, whence on the morning of November 9th it moved forward past our advancing infantry, and after occupying Solre-le-Chateau, an important town of over 3,000 inhabitants, where several prisoners, 1 field-gun, 1 machine gun, a very large ammunition dump and large quantities of rolling stock were captured, pushed on and occupied the villages of Hestrud and Clairfayts, and continued its advance till the Germans were located in a very strong natural position on the east bank of the River Thure. This position, which was practically the line of the Belgian frontier, was then carefully reconnoitred and a full report sent back to Corps Headquarters, and the Regiment then withdrew into Solre-le-Chateau for the night, where it received an enthusiastic welcome from the inhabitants. This was the first successful mounted advance made by the Regiment since 1914. During the day it had made an advance of eight miles on a front of four miles with both flanks exposed, and had made large captures of men and material. For his bold and skilful handling of " A " Squadron on this occasion Lieut. F. F. F. Spicer was awarded an immediate D.S.O., and a large number of officers and men of the Regiment received other immediate awards of different honours. The G.O.C. 13th Corps paid a personal visit to the Regimental Headquarters on 11th November to congratulate the Commanding Officer on the Regiment's work, and subsequently issued the following Order :—" I wish to express to yourself and all ranks of the 12th Lancers my appreciation of the splendid work of the Regiment in the recent operations. The gallantry and the dash displayed, and the excellence of the reports furnished, particularly on the 8th and 9th November, reflect the greatest credit on all concerned, and I am proud to have had you under my command, and am glad that you have had an opportunity of adding to your distinguished record in the final stage of the war." (Signed) Morland, Major-General, Commanding 13th Corps.

The morning following its occupation of Solre-le-Chateau, the Regiment, acting as advanced guard to the South African Infantry Brigade, moved forward again through Hestrud, in the direction of Grandrieu, but the enemy were still holding their overnight positions in strength, and though the advanced troops worked well forward, despite heavy rifle and machine-gun fire, they were ultimately stopped, and an organised infantry attack was then made upon the position. The enemy were, however, strong in artillery, to which we had little reply, as for the past week the Germans had mined and blown up almost every bridge and culvert in their retreat, so that it had only been possible to get a very few guns and a very limited supply of ammunition forward. The South Africans therefore made little progress, in some cases their leading waves not even getting up to where our advanced troops had been checked. Arrangements were made to renew the attack the following morning, and the Regiment, leaving one Squadron just outside Hestrud, was withdrawn to Solre-le-Chateau, where it passed a most unpleasant night, as the Germans shelled the ammunition dump captured the previous day, and a shell at last hitting it, a series of explosions commenced, which continued throughout the night, hundreds of shells going off at a time, shaking the town from end to end with terrific explosions, and belaying it with splinters.

Luckily there were good cellars in most of the buildings, so there were very few casualties, only one man being killed —Sgt. Smith, of " C " Squadron, the last 12th Lancer to be killed in the war. The following morning, November 11th, just as the Regiment was preparing to advance, orders were received that hostilities would cease at 11 a.m., and the war was at an end.

The Regiment moved to Eccles on the afternoon of November 11th, remaining there till November 16th, when it was sent forward in advance of the rest of the army to the town of Philippeville to protect the inhabitants from German soldiers who were reported to be looting there. On arrival the report was found to be false, and the Regiment remained there till the 18th, receiving a most hearty welcome from the inhabitants.

On the 18th it was joined by the remainder of the Brigade, and then moved forward across Belgium, reaching the German frontier on November 24th, and crossing it on December 1st.

A few days later it was sent back into Belgium, where it spent most of the winter very comfortably in Ensival. Demobilization now began, and within a few months only a very small proportion of those officers and men who had so well upheld the honour of the Regiment during the past four years remained with it.

In March, 1919, the Regiment joined the Army of the Rhine in Germany, being quartered in Riehl Barracks, Cologne, till September, 1919, when it proceeded to Ponsonby Barracks, Curragh.

THE RETURN JOURNEY, SEPTEMBER, 1919.

F.Q.M.S. Ashby. Capt. Moore. Major Charrington. Capt. Kellett. A.V.C. S.S.M. Green.

APPENDIX I.

THE BATTLE OF MOY.

On the afternoon of August 28th, 1914, the 5th Cavalry Brigade, composed of the 12th Royal Lancers, 20th Hussars, and the Royal Scots Greys, under the command of Brigadier-General Sir Philip Chetwode, Bart., after reconnoitring in the direction of St. Quentin and finding no trace of the enemy, was withdrawn to the River Oise to water and rest, the Royal Scots Greys furnishing day outposts around Cerizy and the 12th Royal Lancers, who were reserve regiment that day, being sent to the park of the fine chateau on the western edge of the village of Moy. It was a very hot day, and on reaching the park, horses, after being watered, were off-saddled and turned loose to graze, while officers and men had a welcome bathe in the lake, and a shave and wash, for which there had been little opportunity during the three strenuous days preceding. After this, and a visit to the splendid fruit trees the old walled garden of the chateau contained, all ranks settled down to a good and much-needed sleep.

About 4 p.m. shots could be heard from the direction of Cerizy, and Lieut.-Colonel F. Wormald, after giving orders to saddle up at once, galloped with the Adjutant in the direction of the firing to find out what was happening. "C" Squadron, commanded by Captain J. C. Michell, who had saddled up in an incredibly short time, followed a few minutes later with the machine-gun section close behind them. This section, commanded by Lieut. W. R. Styles, was engaged in sorting out all their pack saddlery and equipment when the alarm sounded, but was nevertheless ready for action and on the move in a few minutes.

On reaching the open country north-west of the village, a Squadron of German cavalry could be seen about half a mile away moving in close formation down the hill towards Moy. " C " Squadron were at once dismounted, and, sending their horses back under cover, opened a rapid fire upon the Germans, who at once dismounted, though still upon the forward slope of the hill and completely exposed to our fire.

The accurate fire of " C " Squadron, together with that from our two machine guns, who had now come into action on the flank of " C," caused the German horseholders to let go their horses, which then stampeded, and the dismounted Germans retired back to the crest of the hill and at once began replying to our fire.

" A " and " B " Squadrons had now come up, and were ordered by the Commanding Officer to move under cover to the high ground on the enemy's left flank, and there engage him with dismounted fire.

This manœuvre was admirably executed, and they gained their position quite unseen by the Germans, making excellent use of the cover the many folds in the ground provided, and getting signalling communication with " C " Squadron directly they reached their position.

In the meantime a section of " J " Battery, R.H.A., arrived, and coming into action in rear of the left flank of " C " Squadron, opened an accurate fire upon a small wood just behind the German position, in which there was every reason to suspect were the remaining squadrons of the German regiment we were now opposing.

The Brigadier, who had now arrived on the scene, having been away attending a conference at Corps Headquarters, expressed himself perfectly satisfied with Lieut.-Colonel Wormald's dispositions, and issued further instructions to the Royal Scots Greys and 20th Hussars with a view to dealing with two more regiments of the German Cavalry Brigade which was now discovered to be attacking us. As soon as " A " and " B " Squadrons had reached their position, the Commanding Officer gave " C " Squadron orders to mount, intending to move them forward to a fresh position nearer the enemy, as although the Germans were still maintaining a brisk and accurate fire from the crest of the ridge, the diversion created by the appearance of our two squadrons on their flank would, he thought, enable " C " Squadron to effect a further advance without much difficulty. He also gave the Adjutant, Captain C. E. Bryant, orders to reconnoitre the ground between " C " Squadron and the other two squadrons, and, after ascertaining the exact dispositions of the latter, to return to him.

Captain C. E. Bryant, finding that the ground immediately in front of the German position was so dead that it was possible to approach within fifty yards of them without being seen, actually rode almost on top of the Germans in making certain of the fact, galloped back, and, catching the Commanding Officer moving forward at the head of " C " Squadron, pointed out the wonderful opportunity for a charge. Realizing that by this time the whole of the enemy's attention was concentrated upon the threat to their flank by " A " and " B " Squadrons, the Commanding Officer immediately decided to profit by the occasion. He moved " C " Squadron, who were now in dead ground, just under the ridge the enemy were lining, and then advanced at a walk up the steep ridge in line of troop columns, so as to keep the horses fresh till the last moment. Just before reaching the crest line was formed, and as the Squadron topped the rise " Gallop " and " Charge " were sounded in quick succession by the Regimental Trumpet-Major, and taken up by the " C " Squadron trumpeter. With a ringing cheer, the Squadron charged in perfect line across the fifty yards which now only separated them from the enemy, with the Commanding Officer, his Adjutant, the Trumpet-Major, and two orderlies some twenty yards ahead of them. Though the surprise was complete, the majority of the Germans rose to their feet and fought most gallantly, though a few put up their hands, and others cowered face downwards among the roots they were lying in. The Commanding Officer was immediately wounded, though not before he had transfixed one German with his sword so thoroughly that his sword buckled, and was only extricated later with some difficulty from the man's dead body. One of his orderlies, Private Nolan, was killed, and the other, Private Pacey, had his horse shot under him, but after extricating himself, seized the rifle from a German who was trying to shoot him as he lay under his horse, and not only killed this man, but four other Germans who were close by as well. Trumpet-Major Mowlam, who was following the Commanding Officer, was severely wounded in the thigh, and the only one from the small party of Regimental Headquarters who rode in the charge to come through unscathed was the Adjutant, Captain C. E. Bryant, who personally accounted for no less than five Germans with his own sword.

Captain Michell was instantaneously killed at the head of " C " Squadron as they topped the rise, but otherwise our casualties were amazingly small, four men being killed, and Lieut.-Colonel F. Wormald, and five men wounded. Of this dismounted German squadron, though, hardly a man escaped, over seventy killed and wounded being counted on the ground afterwards, and a few unwounded prisoners being taken.

As soon as " C " Squadron had ridden completely through the German position, they were rallied by Lieut. R. S. W. R. Wyndham-Quin, and charged back again through the position, accounting for the few remaining Germans who were still showing fight, and on reaching the bottom of the hill were once more rallied and brought back over the ground, on which nothing now remained but dead and dying, with the exception of four wounded Germans who were found cowering in the roots, and who were taken prisoners. During this time " A " and " B " Squadrons, supported by the fire from " J " Battery and from our two machine guns, had brought a very effective fire upon the remaining squadrons of the German regiment, who attempted to move forward to their comrades' assistance from the shelter of the little wood already referred to.

Our accurate fire, however, soon sent them back in disorder. A fresh German regiment which appeared a little later was dealt with in a similarly effective manner, and " C " Squadron were thus enabled to reform and collect their wounded quite unmolested by the enemy.

Throughout the engagement the Royal Scots Greys and 20th Hussars had been successfully engaging the remaining regiments of this German Cavalry Brigade, which was afterwards discovered to be commanded by the Prince von Furstenburg. The 20th Hussars, with their accurate rifle fire, silenced a German battery which attempted to come into action almost before it fired a single round, and the Royal Scots Greys backed up the charge of " C " Squadron with a mounted squadron. Both these regiments inflicted very heavy casualties upon the enemy, and this brigade, it is now known, suffered so severely in this day's action that it was withdrawn into reserve, and took no part in the German advance for several days.

The whole action exemplified almost as well as could be desired the successful combination of fire and shock action, and the value of our pre-war training both with rifle and lance. The steadiness of a squadron that in the heat of mounted action could quickly rally not once but twice and immediately carry out a fresh mission, as " C " Squadron had done, could hardly be equalled ; and the co-operation of the other two squadrons, and of the section of " J " Battery and the machine guns, could not have been improved upon.

The German regiment engaged was the 2nd (Queen Victoria's Own) Prussian Dragoons, and it was ascertained later that its Commanding Officer and most of its Headquarter staff had been with the dismounted squadron, and had been killed in the charge.

The actual charge took place in the vicinity of Cerizy, but to all ranks in the 12th Royal Lancers it will always be known as the Battle of Moy.

APPENDIX II.

Reports on Operations East of Amiens, March 30th, 1918.

From G.O.C. 9th Australian Infantry Brigade to Headquarters, 6th Division.

I beg to forward herewith detailed report of counter-attack operations carried out by 9th Australian Infantry Brigade on afternoon and evening of March 30th.

The assistance rendered by 12th Royal Lancers, 2nd Cavalry Division, was invaluable, and my officers and men are enthusiastic of the work done by the Cavalry.

Extract from above report:—" The 12th Royal Lancers preceded the battalion and reached wood east of Bois-de-Hangard at about 4.15 p.m. This wood will in future be referred to as Lancer Wood. On our way to Lancer Wood, we passed several bodies of troops peculiarly and uselessly entrenched in queer places, and large parties of stragglers.

On reaching the wood, we found the whole front-line garrison withdrawing, although there was no hostile fire of any kind and no signs of attack. I met two Brigadiers and a Battalion Commander in the wood and informed them of what was happening, and asked that they should get their men back to the line at once. This they promised to do.

The Cavalry Commander also helped in the matter by sending a squadron dismounted to re-establish their line. The infantry then went forward with the cavalry, but in a reluctant manner. During the whole time we went forward men were constantly leaving the line, and there seemed to be no effort to stop this straggling.

It was a proud privilege to be allowed to work with such a fine regiment as the 12th Royal Lancers. Their approach march instilled in the men the utmost confidence and enthusiasm, and, I am glad to say, did much to counteract the effect of the straggling.

They lost no time in effectively clearing Lancer Wood, and got there just in time, as the enemy had gained a footing in the southern and south-east edges of the wood. Their action now allowed us to move forward to the attack.

On seeing the cavalry there, the enemy shelled Lancer Wood very heavily with 5.9's, paying particular attention to the outer fringes. Fairly heavy casualties to horses were inflicted, and the horses were soon led from the wood to a position west of Villers-Bretonneux—Aubercourt road.

The discipline shown during this heavy shelling was an object-lesson.

During our attack the cavalry protected both our flanks, the left with Hotchkiss guns. They withdrew at about 7 p.m. All ranks were eager to give every possible help, and throughout there was wholehearted co-operation.

The experience gained in this our first operation with cavalry was invaluable. One was able to judge of the splendid work they are doing for the army at the present time, and they cannot be too highly praised.

(Signed) L. MORSHEAD, Lieut.-Colonel,
Commanding 31st Australian Infantry Battalion.

Report from G.O.C. 5th Cavalry Brigade.

A report on the counter-attack operations carried out by the 9th Australian Infantry Brigade has been received. In it the G.O.C. 9th Australian Infantry Brigade expresses his appreciation in enthusiastic terms of the fine work of the 12th Royal Lancers, who acted in co-operation with this attack. The G.O.C. 5th Cavalry Brigade wishes to record afresh his pride in having the 12th Royal Lancers under his command, and considers that the Regiment has won fresh honours for itself and the Brigade by earning the appreciation in action of such gallant comrades as the 9th Australian Infantry Brigade.

(Signed) W. F. COLLINS, Lieut.-Colonel,
Commanding 5th Cavalry Brigade.

APPENDIX III.

Disembarked at Havre, August 17th, 1914.

Strength of Regiment on Disembarkation.—Officers, 25; other ranks, 523; horses, 608.

Reinforcements to November 11th, 1918.—Officers, 85; other ranks, 1,124; horses, 1,688.

CASUALTIES.

Officers.—Killed, 12; wounded, 30.

Other Ranks.—Killed, 110; wounded and missing, 430.

The following honours have been won by Officers, W.Os., N.C.Os., and men of the Regiment :—

Officers.		*Other Ranks*	
C.B.	2	D.C.M.	11
C.M.G.	2	M.M.	25
O.B.E.	1	M.S.M.	5
Brevets	6	Russian Medals ...	3
D.S.O.	6	French Medals ...	3
D.S.O. and bar ...	1	Italian Medals	1
M.C.	18	Belgian Medal	1
M.C. and bar	2	Rumanian Medal ...	1
French Medals... ...	5	Mention	6
Egyptian Medal ...	1	Divisional Cards ...	30
Mentions	43		

Forty-seven other ranks of the Regiment obtained permanent commissions, out of which—

1 rose to the rank of Lieutenant-Colonel,
1 ,, ,, ,, Major,
12 ,, ,, ,, Captain,
33 ,, ,, ,, Lieutenant,

and gained the following honours :—

D.S.O. and bar ...	1	M.C.	11
D.S.O.	1	O.B.E.	1
M.C. and bar	1	Croix de Guerre ...	1

Twenty-seven other ranks of the Regiment obtained temporary commissions.

NOMINAL ROLL OF OFFICERS AND OTHER RANKS KILLED AND DIED OF WOUNDS.

RANK.	NAME.		REMARKS.
Brig./Gen.	Wormald, F., C.B.	...	Killed in action, 3/10/1915.
Major	Crawley, E. ...	...	,, ,, 2/11/1914.
Captain	Michell, J. C. ...	...	,, ,, 10/9/1914.
,,	Murray, F. W. S.	...	,, ,, 30/10/1914.
Lieut.	Leatham, E. H.	...	,, ,, 31/10/1914.
,,	Eden, J.	...	,, ,, 17/10/1914.
2/Lieut.	Wroughton, M. C.	...	Died of wounds, 31/10/1914.
Lieut.	Gordon, G. ...	...	Killed in action, 30/4/1915.
,,	Brown, G. M., M.C.	...	,, ,, 28/11/1917.
2/Lieut.	Hammond, A. E.	...	,, ,, 28/11/1917.
Lieut.	Palmer, H. ...	...	,, ,, 2/10/1918.
Captain	Yeatherd, M. L.	...	,, ,, 11/4/1917.
Lieut./Col.	Wood, R. B. ...	...	,, ,, —/8/1918.

No.	RANK.	NAME.		REMARKS.
713	L./Cpl.	London, J. ...	...	Killed in action, 23/8/1914.
127	Pte.	Hunt, C. H. ...	...	,, ,, 23/8/1914.
3897	L./Cpl.	Totman, W. W.	...	Died of wounds, 26/8/1914.
4458	Cpl.	Gore, H. ...	...	Killed in action, 28/8/1914.
2825	Pte.	Hunt, D. ...	...	,, ,, 28/8/1914.
1746	,,	Nolan, H. ...	...	,, ,, 28/8/1914.
4873	S.Q.M.S.	Tompkins, E. J.	...	,, ,, 28/8/1914.
1561	Pte.	Coote, C. ...	...	,, ,, 28/8/1914.
5198	,,	Farrow, E. F. ...	...	,, ,, 6/9/1914.
4308	,,	Waters, W. J. ...	...	,, ,, 6/9/1914.
4682	,,	Auker, S. J. ...	...	,, ,, 23/8/1914.
3736	,,	Collar, J. W. ...	...	,, ,, 23/8/1914.
4188	,,	Johnson, F. W.	...	,, ,, 23/8/1914.
332	,,	Plant, G. F. ...	...	,, ,, 23/8/1914.
3280	L./Cpl.	Chapman, H. ...	...	,, ,, 10/9/1914.
5896	Pte.	Dudman, E. ...	...	,, ,, 10/9/1914.
5562	Sgt.	Kempster, W. H.	...	,, ,, 10/9/1914.
399	Pte.	Pryce, W. ...	...	,, ,, 10/9/1914.
3355	,,	Reynolds, W. S.	...	,, ,, 10/9/1914.
3418	,,	Smith, J. G. ...	...	Prisoner of war, date and place of death unknown.
3629	L./Cpl.	Knight, H. ...	...	Died of wounds, 28/8/1914.
2510	Pte.	Smith, H. A. ...	...	Wounded and missing, believed killed, 14/9/1914.
417	,,	Hart, F. ...	...	Prisoner of war, died of wounds, 25/10/1914.

No.	Rank.	Name.	Remarks.
213	Pte.	Duggan, G. J.	Died of wounds, 21/10/1914.
1576	,,	Savage, P. J.	Killed in action, 21/10/1914.
4403	L./Cpl.	Crayston, R. A. N.	Died of wounds, 31/10/1914.
609	Cpl.	Wingate, G.	,, ,, 1/11/1914.
138	,,	Robinson, T.	Killed in action, 1/11/1914.
2085	Pte.	Welsh, P.	,, ,, 1/11/1914.
5223	S.S.	Giddings, M. W.	Died of wounds, 2/11/1914.
1675	Pte.	Cooper, T. G.	,, ,, 8/11/1914.
1711	,,	Webb, S. H.	Killed in action, 1/11/1914.
4332	,,	Fryer, R.	,, ,, 11/11/1914.
4206	,,	Duncan, F. J.	,, ,, 11/11/1914.
906	Cpl.	Bell, T.	,, ,, 20/11/1914.
1302	Pte.	Evans, G.	,, ,, 20/11/1914.
3084	,,	McCann, M.	,, ,, 20/11/1914.
5920	,,	Rogers, W.	,, ,, 20/11/1914.
1294	Cpl.	Westell, F.	,, ,, 20/11/1914
4528	Pte.	Barnes, J. E.	Died of wounds, 25/11/1914.
1444	L./Cpl.	Graham, W. J	Killed in action, 21/2/1915.
3246	Pte.	Wheeldon, H.	Died of wounds, 22/2/1915.
2992	,,	Crook, G. T.	,, ,, 23/2/1915.
3882	L./Cpl.	Jackson, J. A.	Killed in action, 23/2/1915.
5833	Pte.	Norman, H.	Died of wounds, 24/2/1915.
1668	L./Cpl.	Robinson, H.	Accidentally killed, 19/3/1915
133	Pte.	Mayne, G. H.	Killed in action, 2/5/1915.
1480	,,	Greendale, A.	Died of sickness, 16/5/1915.
5868	,,	Baker, A.	Killed in action, 16/5/1915.
1536	,,	Smith, H.	,, ,, 17/5/1915.
5483	,,	Holmes, A. A.	Died of wounds, 17/5/1915.
1289	,,	Jenkins, G.	,, ,, 17/5/1915.
5355	,,	Forsey, F.	Killed in action, 18/5/1915.
137	,,	New, F. V.	,, ,, 18/5/1915.
405	,,	Lock, J.	,, ,, 21/5/1915.
439	,,	Sevior, A. E.	Died of wounds, 21/5/1915.
5175	,,	Surridge, —.	,, ,, 8/6/1915.
5807	L./Cpl.	Allen, S.	,, ,, (date unknown).
4173	Pte.	Robb, J. F. H.	Accidentally drowned, 15/9/1915.
6353	,,	Phillips, H. A.	Killed in action, 31/1/1916.
6341	,,	Newbury, H.	,, ,, 3/2/1916.
404	,,	Sheppard, F. A.	,, ,, 3/2/1916.
8588	,,	Sayles, G. W.	Died of wounds, 4/2/1916.
7642	,,	Taylor, F.	,, ,, 3/6/1916.
5564	,,	Palmer, A. E.	,, ,, 11/9/1916.
4745	L./Cpl.	Surman, B.	Accidentally killed, 11/11/1916
3226	Pte.	Barnard, C. J.	Died of sickness, 30/1/1917.
620	,,	Madgewick, F.	,, ,, 2/3/1917.
5863	,,	Davies, J. A.	Killed in action, 10/4/1917.

No.	Rank.	Name.	Remarks.
5495	Pte.	Pipkin, T. H.	Killed in action, 11/4/1917.
3080	L./Cpl.	Pheiffer, W. J.	,, ,, 11/4/1917.
3307	Pte.	Reed, A. J.	,, ,, 11/4/1917.
5988	,,	Stanley, A. E.	Died of wounds, 14/4/1917.
5810	,,	Walker, W.	Killed in action, 11/4/1917.
6478	,,	Raven, F.	,, ,, 11/4/1917.
4450	,,	Brading, A.	,, ,, 11/4/1917.
1673	,,	Beadle, F.	,, ,, 10/4/1917.
16098	,,	Fox, C. E.	,, ,, 10/4/1917.
5721	,,	Read, F.	Died of wounds, 10/4/1917.
412	,,	Sutton, J.	Killed in action, 9/4/1917.
5171	Cpl.	Williams, H. J.	Died of wounds, 15/4/1917.
6466	L./Cpl.	Pickering, J. W.	,, ,, 2/5/1917.
5917	Cpl.	Poulter, P.	,, ,, 25/5/1917.
1042	Pte.	Holbrook, P.	Killed in action, 30/5/1917.
4617	,,	Pilley, E.	Died of wounds, 1/6/1917.
5136	Sgt.	Thompson, J.	,, ,, 29/6/1917.
5872	Pte.	Waghorn, C.	Killed in action, 25/11/1917.
3605	Tptr.	Stallard, A. E.	,, ,, 28/11/1917.
16024	Pte.	Williams, A.	,, ,, 28/11/1917.
409	Sgt.	Edwards, B. P., D.C.M.	Died of wounds, 28/11/1917.
11144	L./Cpl.	Barrett, G. F.	Killed in action, 28/11/1917.
536	Pte.	Cummings, H.	,, ,, 28/11/1917.
4456	,,	Groves, A.	,, ,, 30/11/1917.
4730	,,	Barnwell, S.	,, ,, 30/11/1917.
5501	,,	Corquin, T.	,, ,, 29/11/1917.
4267	Sgt.	Phillips, H.	Died of wounds, 5/12/1917.
6533	Pte.	Francis, P. A.	,, ,, 19/12/1917.
8164	,,	Kennaird, W.	,, ,, 26/12/1917.
6858	L./Cpl.	Baker, J.	Killed in action, 27/1/1918.
4054	Pte.	Mackay, E. J.	Died of wounds, 27/3/1918.
13005	Sgt.	Tomkinson, E.	,, ,, 27/3/1918.
10014	Pte.	Hill, C. R.	,, ,, 23/3/1918.
5833	,,	Howard, W. F.	,, ,, 23/3/1918.
12959	L./Cpl.	Wilson, W.	,, ,, 30/3/1918.
3620	S.S.	Cooper, J. H.	,, ,, 31/3/1918.
5569	L./Cpl.	George, E.	Killed in action, 21/3/1918.
5208	,,	Seconde, A. H.	,, ,, 23/3/1918.
8195	Pte.	Spencer, J.	,, ,, 23/3/1918.
1942	,,	Rogers, E. H.	,, ,, 25/3/1918.
1286	,,	Crowther, P.	,, ,, 30/3/1918.
1298	,,	Lovett, G.	,, ,, 30/3/1918.
8288	L./Cpl.	Turner, G. H.	,, ,, 30/3/1918.
12873	Pte.	Lee, G.	Died of wounds, 31/3/1918.
11404	,,	Peacock, W.	Killed in action, 1/4/1918.
9963	,,	Draper, J. W.	,, ,, 1/4/1918.
7662	L./Cpl.	Murray, H. E.	Died of wounds, 3/4/1918.
11437	Pte.	Shawley, T. W.	,, ,, 4/4/1918.

No.	Rank.	Name.	Remarks.
12898	Pte.	Denton, J. J.	Died of wounds, 13/4/1918.
1660	„	Eldridge, L.	Died of sickness, 5/7/1918.
917	„	Milnes, F. E.	Died whilst prisoner of war, 24/6/1918.
2168	Sgt./Tptr.	Stallard, F. W. ...	Killed in action, 2/10/1918.
708	Pte.	Horsley, A. E. ...	Died of wounds, 9/10/1918.
10515	„	Crickett, —.	Killed in action, 12/10/1918.
12950	Sgt.	Smith, —.	„ „ 10/11/1918.

NOMINAL ROLL OF OFFICERS WHO SERVED WITH THE REGIMENT DURING THE PERIOD AUGUST 17TH, 1914—NOVEMBER 11TH, 1918.

RANK AND NAME.	DATE OF JOINING.
Lt.-Col. (Brig.-Gen.) F. Wormald, C.B.	Disembarked with Regiment, 17/8/14.
Major E. Crawley	,, ,, ,,
Major P. J. Bailey, D.S.O.	,, ,, ,,
Major (Brig.-Gen.) B. Macnaghten, D.S.O.	,, ,, ,,
Major (Lt.-Col.) C. Fane, C.M.G., D.S.O.	,, ,, ,,
Capt. J. C. Michell	,, ,, ,,
Capt. F. W. S. Murray	,, ,, ,,
Capt. (Major) W. B. Bell	,, ,, ,,
Capt. H. Colmore (7th Hussars) ...	,, ,, ,,
Lt. & Adjt. (Maj.) C. E. Bryant, D.S.O.	,, ,, ,,
Lt. (Major) H. V. S. Charrington, M.C.	,, ,, ,,
Lt. (Capt.) B. G. Nicholas	,, ,, ,,
Lt. E. H. Leatham	,, ,, ,,
Lt. (Major) W. R. Styles, M.C. ...	,, ,, ,,
Lt. (Capt.) R. S. W. R. Wyndham-Quin M.C.	,, ,, ,,
Lt. (Capt.) D. C. H. Richardson, M.C.	,, ,, ,,
Lt. J. Eden	,, ,, ,,
Lt. (Capt.) R. S. T. Moore	,, ,, ,,
2/Lt. (T./Major) H. A. Wernher ...	,, ,, ,,
2/Lt. (T./Capt.) A. P. Boden, M.C. ...	,, ,, ,,
2/Lt. (T./Capt.) H. A. F. Brand ...	,, ,, ,,
Lt. (T./Capt.) J. H. Leche	,, ,, ,,
2/Lieut. M. C. Wroughton	,, ,, ,,
Lt. & Qmr. (Major) H. B. Knop ...	,, ,, ,,
Capt. H. Bone (A.V.C.)	,, ,, ,,
Capt. H. G. Gibson (R.A.M.C.) ...	,, ,, ,,
Capt. (Lt.-Col.) C. H. G. Black, D.S.O.	Joined Regiment 17/9/14.
2/Lt. Sir B. Pigott, Bart.	,, ,, ,,
Major Hon. H. G. Heneage, D.S.O. ...	,, ,, 22/9/14.
Capt. G. B. Ollivant	,, ,, 30/9/14.
2/Lt. (Lt.) W. J. Baird	,, ,, 15/11/14.
Capt. A. L. Browne	,, ,, 24/11/14.
Lt. (Capt.) P. J. Davidson	,, ,, 10/11/14.
Lt. J. R. C. Rawnsley, M.C.	,, ,, 28/10/14.
Capt. (T./Lt.-Col.) T. R. Badger ...	Disembarked with Regiment, 17/8/14.

Rank and Name.	Date of Joining.
2/Lt. (Major) J. Leslie, D.S.O., M.C. ...	Joined Regiment 29/9/14.
Lt. H. Montgomery	Disembarked with Regiment, 17/8/14.
Lt. G. Gordon	Joined Regiment 10/11/14.
Lt. A. H. Williams (C. I. H.) ...	" " 17/9/14.
2/Lt. (Lt.) C. Hart (from ranks) ...	Disembarked with Regiment, 17/8/14.
2/Lt. (Lt.) R. E. Vine (from ranks) ...	" " "
2/Lt. (Lt.) F. F. F. Spicer, D.S.O. ...	Joined Regiment 10/11/14.
Lt. G. M. Brown, M.C.	" " 29/1/15.
Major (Lt.-Col.) C. M. Truman, D.S.O.	" " 31/12/14.
2/Lt. (T./Capt.) C. B. Ismay	" " 17/3/15.
2/Lt. (Lt.) P. M. L. Edmunds ...	" " 23/1/15.
Lt. V. L. C. Manning	" " 13/2/15.
2/Lt. (Lt.) Hon. B. A. A. Ogilvy, M.C.	" " 7/5/15.
Lt. J. J. G. Keppell (A.V.C.)	" " 18/4/15.
Capt. H. B. Dickson (R.A.M.C.) ...	" " 30/5/15.
T./Lieut. (T./Capt.) D. Kennedy, M.C. (R.A.M.C.)	" 3/4/17.
Major A. B. Reynolds, D.S.O. ...	" " 1/7/15.
Capt. M. F. Murray	" " 25/8/15.
2/Lt. (Lt.) P. R. Astley, M.C. ...	" " 27/9/15.
2/Lt. (Lt.) A. S. C. Browne	" " 30/9/15.
2/Lt. (Lt.) A. A. McBean	" " 22/10/15.
2/Lt. (Lt.) A. V. Grimes (from ranks)	" " 22/8/14.
2/Lt. (Lt.) R. Straker, M.C.	" " 12/11/15.
2/Lt. (Lt.) C. de V. Harding (from ranks, 2nd Dgns.)	" 20/10/15.
Lt. D. N. Savile-Stewart, M.C. ...	" " 22/12/15.
2/Lt. (Lt.) R. L. McCreery, M.C. ...	" " 30/12/15.
2/Lt. (Lt.) Hon. K. McKay	" " "
2/Lt. (Lt.) M. H. O'Rorke	" " 8/8/15.
2/Lt. (Capt.) W. Vass, M.C. (from ranks)	" " 4/2/16.
2/Lt. (T./Lt.) C. V. A. Cartwright ...	" " "
2/Lt. (T./Lt.) E. A. W. Barron, M.C.	" " "
2/Lt. S. K. Gwyer	" " "
2/Lt. J. Hope-Nelson	" " "
2/Lt. (T./Lt.) G. H. Freer	" " 5/3/16.
Lt. C. C. L. Williams, M.C.	" " 31/7/16.
2/Lt. (T/Lt.) G. W. MacIlwaine ...	" " "
Capt. (Major) W. L. C. Kirby, D.S.O.	" " 2/9/16.
2/Lt. A. E. Hammond	" " 27/9/16.
2/Lt. (T./Capt.) A. F. Davidge, M.C. (from ranks)	Disembarked with Regiment, 17/8/14.
2/Lt. (Lt.) H. Palmer (from ranks) ...	" " "
Capt. M. L. Yeatherd	Joined Regiment, 13/10/16.
Capt. C. C. Lister	" " "
Capt. (Major) H. C. Maydon	" " 7/11/16.
2/Lieut. W. E. Ford	" " 3/1/17.
2/Lt. (T./Lt.) H. M. B. Chester ...	" " "

Rank and Name.	Date of Joining.
2/Lt. (T./Lt.) J. S. Scott	Joined Regiment 10/1/17.
2/Lt. H. A. Lamb	,, ,, ,,
2/Lt. (T./Lt.) C. K. Olney	,, ,, 20/1/17.
2/Lt. A. Angus	,, ,, ,,
2/Lt. (Lt.) N. L. Mackinnon	,, ,, 14/1/17.
2/Lt. (Lt.) F. Mylrea	,, ,, 23/2/17.
2/Lt. (T./Lt.) J. W. Bennett	,, ,, ,,
2/Lt. (T./Lt.) E. Gould	,, ,, ,,
Capt. J. A. Purdey	,, ,, 7/5/17.
2/Lt. (Lt.) R. G. Goldsmid	,, ,, 5/8/17.
Lt. W. O. Berryman, M.C.	,, ,, 25/10/17.
2/Lt. (T./Lt.) W. Monks	,, ,, 21/10/17.
T./Lt. (Major) J. Hickey, O.B.E. ...	,, ,, 4/12/17.
2/Lt. (T./Capt.) L. Williams	,, ,, 6/1/18.
2/Lt. (T./Lt.) H. Hudson	,, ,, ,,
2/Lt. (T./Lt.) R. Bullen	,, ,, 14/1/18.
2/Lt. (T./Lt.) C. P. Beaven	,, ,, ,,
2/Lt. (Lt.) C. A. Morris	,, ,, 9/12/18.
T./Lt. W. T. Harvey	,, ,, 10/3/18.
2/Lt. H. W. Thorley	,, ,, 24/2/18.
2/Lt. J. Marshall	,, ,, 1/3/18.
Lt. G. P. Williams	,, ,, 6/4/18.
Capt. J. V. Adair, M.C. (N.I.H.) ...	,, ,, 22/4/18.
2/Lt. J. Sturrock	,, ,, 25/4/18.
Lt. E. W. Cooper	,, ,, 28/4/18.
Lt. A. T. Campbell	,, ,, ,,
2/Lt. D. J. Turville	,, ,, 30/4/18.
2/Lt. W. A. Stratford	,, ,, 6/4/18.
2/Lt. D. I. Morgans, M.C.	,, ,, ,,
2/Lt. H. Richards, M.C.	,, ,, 15/4/18.
2/Lt. D. P. Jones	,, ,, 19/6/18.
Lt. and Qmr. W. Domone (from ranks)	Disembarked with Regiment, 17/8/14.
2/Lt. D. Raby	Joined Regiment 19/6/18.
2/Lt. W. C. C. King	,, ,, 28/6/18.
Lt. R. H. Evans	,, ,, 25/10/18.
Lt. F. T. Baines	,, ,, ,,
Lt. J. N. M. Fraser	,, ,, ,,